What I Can Tell You

Ruth Moon Kempher —i

What I Can Tell You

Poems by Ruth Moon Kempher

Bright Hill Press

Treadwell, New York
2013

What I Can Tell You

Poems by Ruth Moon Kempher

Bright Hill Press Poetry Award Series, No. 19
2012 Winner - Chosen by Philip Mosley

Cover Art and Book Design by Bertha Rogers
Editor in Chief: Bertha Rogers
Assistant Editor: Lawrence E. Shaw
Editorial Intern: Marlise Cammer

Library of Congress Cataloging-in-Publication Data

Kempher, Ruth Moon.
  [Poems. Selections]
  What I can tell you : poems / by Ruth Moon Kempher.
     pages ; cm.
  ISBN 978-1-892471-72-7 (alk. paper)
  I. Title.

PS3561.E42W47 2013
811'.54--dc23

2013013794

What I Can Tell You is published by Bright Hill Press. Bright Hill Press,
Inc., a non-for-profit, 501 (c) (3) literary and educational organization,
was founded in 1992. The organization is registered with the New York
State Department of State, Office of Charities Registration. Publication
of *What I Can Tell You* is made possible, in part, with public funds from
the Literature Program of the New York State Council on the Arts and
with the support of Governor Andrew Cuomo and the New York State
Legislature.

Editorial Address:
Bright Hill Press, Inc., 94 Church Street
Treadwell, NY 13846
Voice: 607-829-5055; Fax: 607-829-5054
Website: www.brighthillpress.org
E-mail: wordthur@stny.rr.com

Acknowledgements

Some of these poems have appeared, sometimes in a different
form and / or under a different title, in the following
journals and anthologies:

Abbey:"Mimosa Trees: A Thank You,"
"Moment Apocalyptic," "Descending Now"
Argestes: "How Gulley Jimson's Adam Isn't Mine"
Bogg: "Northeast Wind: Separations"
Bosco: "Buying a New Mattress"
Caprice: "Saturday Started Early, 2:11 a. m.,"
"Of Keys and Time"
Casa de Cinco Hermanas: "Drawing Lesson: Balloons,"
"History TheyWant"
Chiron Review: "Her Explanation,"
"Waiting for the Dempsey Dumpster Man,"
"At Bowling, Monday Night," "*Commedia dell'Arte*, Too Late"
Earth's Daughters: "Of Dogs and Heaven,"
"Notes for a Letter or a Sculpture"
Edgz: "Directive: DO NOT GO TO BATAVIA,"
"Near Midnight, Cuna Street"
Ekphrasis: "'The Lovers'—A Painting by Remedios Varo,"
"Portrait: Untitled"
Exit 13: "Old Ties for the Asking," "Nostalgia. . ."
"Journal Entry: November 7"
5 A. M.: "At Scrabble, One Night"
Florida Review: "Wayside Flowers, Well," *"Getaway"*
Home Planet News: "How the House Moves with the Morning"
Hurricane Review: "Looms: A Digression"
Journal of New Jersey Poets: "Of Beaches," "Cycle for J. Miro. . ."
"At Ninety-seven, My Dad"
Kalliope: "The Kohler Ad"
Lilliput: "The Sidewalk Artist's Legacy"
Many Mountains Moving: "Zones and Circles, Love"
Marjorie Kinnan Rawlings Journal of Florida Literature:
"Of Trees—with D. H. L. . .," "Of Bees"
Minotaur: "The Hybridizer Crows," "Arabesque"
Off the Coast: "Object of Affliction: The Thistle"
Pearl: "Post Cards from the Nation's Oldest City,"
"What I Can Tell You Is"
Pinyon Review: "The Purist of Pear Trees"
Presa: "In a Land of Small Rain"

Ruth Moon Kempher —vii

Contents

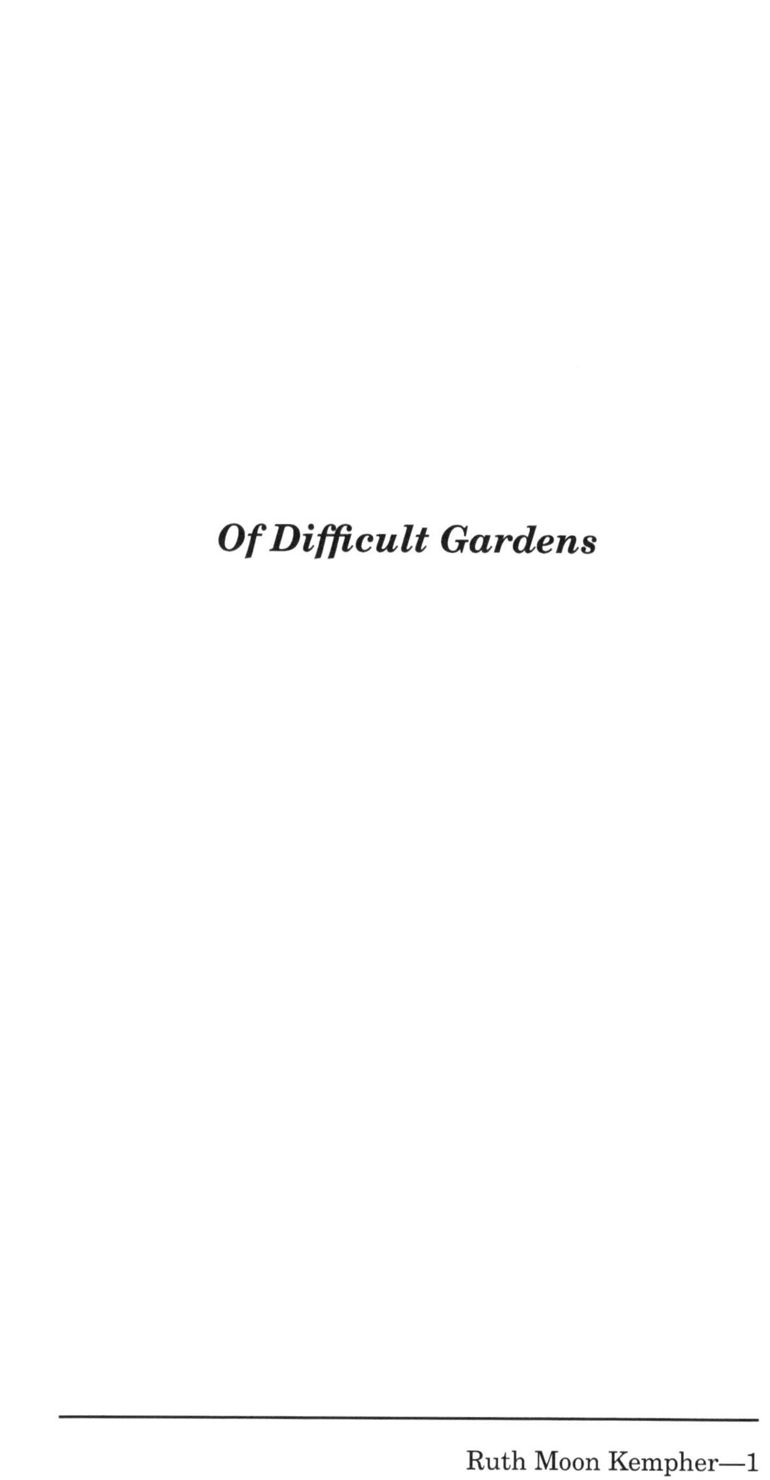

Of Difficult Gardens

Wayside Flowers, Well

I will sing, as doth behove,
Hymns in praise of what I love!

—William Wordsworth,
"To the Small Celandine"

First there were fist-sized
lotus, gasping
in the murk, pond
at the obsessive artist's
(he more interested
in 13th Century tiles
            than in how
his lilies groped
for a living)
            but then
at St. Winifred's Well, in
Woolston, Shropshire
where we almost fell in
laughing, there were
                yellows
(Chris said, "Surely
that's celandine") tiny
yellow poppies
in a maze, amazing, well—
those waters are supposed
by the local gentry
to cure lameness—dark
waters, curding up

                (Winifred's bones
rested here, they say, on
their sacred journey) but
there was such laughter
                about the words
"Flower," like "plougher"
and "Flow-er," the Well
O, O, the Well flows
                lovely
                gives root-room
in treacherous slime
among well-stones, to
the tiny shining stars—
the celandine.

In A Land of Small Rain

Wooden, and other objects—
knuckles of maple, or the oaks' bones—
all wait on the small rain to drop
merciful, from the heavens.
Larch dog and cedar kitten, moss-laden
impinge on yesterday drought-stricken
as somewhere past the hot horizon
chips of tulip fall away, revealing
a fashionable salmon, or
a cherry herring. . . their roots
tangled with worms, thirst together
knotted like seines.
It's a burly world as old, ripe sap
dries into beads thick as honey—traps
for gnats and spiders—the rain's
absence felt tangible as present sun.
Trickles of sawdust dry the palms—
a small wind stirs the pines
and rustles the palmettos.
Here, grief grows deep
like a hardwood hooked into earth—
waits, as its roots tap brine.

A Judas Noon

Something's eating the figtree. Giant hoppers
in the grass eye—haunch-sprung like pterodactyls
trembling taut on bone hinges—anything green.
Stems. Something's hungry for figs. But it's
too hot for croquet; and poems are not damp enough
nor gin. Not today. Feasting on leaves, whatever
slakes that gnawing need, some ragged creature has
made lace here, waving fanlike over jeweled fish
mired in pool muck too unglazed to mirror the lilies.

Then comes this minor sermon: a breath of rain.

Who Was Contrary in the Garden
Wasn't Mary

Hoe-handed, busy, row by row, she jokes
about how she's grown older; jests of beans
and bluebells, Queen Anne's lace—she's seen
eternities of each, she says, but never speaks
derisively of clover. Sometimes in waking dreams
she sees an ogre, she tells me, a bee-trapper—
that short-ribbed giant who brought her orchids
panting for her promise. Never again, she vows.
An older woman doesn't fall for honey.
She insists I tell the trolls that penny roses
cost thirteen cents a dozen now; the hound's-
tooth violets, a dime. It's just a matter
of survival. You'll see, she swears, he'll miss
my cockle shells, the flowered bed he left behind.

Object of Affliction:
The Thistle

           is, speaking in tongues
a lisp of nasty business, having been
picked here, for its ill nature
or rather, once
having been plucked
into one's pocket, it's a ticklish
situation, but I digress.
           They're purple
of course, dancing wind-struck
in certain Tchaikovskian
suites, as Russian Cossacks—
green boots that click and stomp
           in a fantasia's chorus
serrated frond-hands awaver—
whose music is impossible
to disremember.
           Bristle-topped
they stick around—
too ephemeral to persevere
forever, too multiple
to stop.

Correspondence

Of Beaches

Your beach. . . reminds me of San Francisco,
Santa Cruz, Half Moon Bay, Pacifica. . . beaches
with the wry smiles.
　　　　　—Tom Plante, Editor of *Exit 13*, in a letter

as if writing of the local weather, his "wry smiles" of beaches pleases my
lips into an answering sort of chuckle, and that word now, "chuckle" is
what my beaches did, at their best— that burble of surf insinuating its
waters into drift—
old seaweed tangled pieces of bottle, shell—
you name it, if fishers or swimmers or lovers can bring it
　　　　　　　　　　it more than likely is left
　　　　　　　　　　to make music, at best. . .

but then there's his list. San Francisco?
Just north, if I remember correctly, is Stinson Beach
and in the way past. . . what I think of is distant breakers
coming in, swirling, frigid water, and the boy with me
teased 'til I swam out too far, foundered, he later
　　　　　　　　　　called me a bitch
　　　　　　　　　　and my mother was not amused—

I probably giggled. Certainly shivered. Santa Cruz?
I don't think I've ever been there, and of Half Moon Bay, admit
I stayed aboard ship, anchored out on the deep azure ripples
preferring to skip falling into a tender, wobbly and woozy
just to attend a corporate shindig. . .
　　　　　　　　　　and of my own beach? the question
　　　　　　　　　　is which?

Pacifica? Never. Nor Gulf Coast. It's been the Atlantic always.
Atlantic Highlands, on the Jersey shore dumped my small self into
terror of water, seemed like forever, 'til I came alive in it
up on our north beach, where the house fell in, in nightmares
or south, walking dogs, dreaming we'd have the run of it
                         forever. . . forgot to remember
                         sea change—all moved on.

Postcards, From the Nation's Oldest City

1.

The cobblestones of Charlotte Street are
haunted; Eve the other day was heard as she
poked her head in at Coco Mickler's smithy
saying to Coco—barrel-chested and lame
blacksmith reminiscent of a certain pounder
of lightening bolts & a wicked wife—O maybe
Venus got away with a bunch because of
that limp, always a quick answer from some

2.

what Eve said, squinting in the smoky
interior was "Don't blame it on me, Baby.
If it hadn't been me picked that apple, or
as some people want it, that pomegranate—
but whoever heard of pomegranate pie?—
it would have been one of my daughters, or
worse, one of those bitches from over those
hills, yonder, come from nowhere to seduce
my boys. Or any woman half alive

3.

& being intrigued by the true nature of
life. As I grow older, I tend to confuse
the worm in the apple with the snake, which
confirms the lessening of us all, apparently.”

If I
didn't love you or someone, I wouldn't be
writing this now. Did you know my Daddy
was a Baptist minister once, who sang tenor
in a strong melodic voice, all the hymns, like
“I come to the Garden alone, and the dew

4.

is still on the roses; and He walks with me
and He talks with me, and He tells me I am
His own,” only later occurred to me that's
very sexy lyrics, if as it were they were sung
Sarah V or Ella Fitzgerald. O Lord, I walked
down Charlotte Street early one morning—
the dew was still on the Dempsey Dumpster
across from The Tradewinds, and some bum
was in it, with his feet wagging up in the air
skiving for tin cans, maybe, bottles—

5.

this young guy Ra was with me and I liked
the way he talked and how the gone-almost
stars meshed and spun over the haunted
as I said before cobbles. And I was just
thinking to add to the haunting, when
two or ten things at once occurred to me:
I had turned my back on the century plant
at the corner, which is not good to pass
without a greeting, and by walking down
Charlotte past the blacksmith's, I was

6.

walking toward the Plaza and King Street
stepping back toward that damned statue of
supercilious Ponce de Leon, his swagger
stick and plumed hat from some other Sunday
how those funnies smelled of fresh ink and
the cold taste of ice cream cones from the drug-
                                    store
and those other shadows, thinking also how
we see each other in the light of shadows, or
as creatures of each other's dreams.

Notes for a Letter, or Sculpture

   April again, the trees showed their bone
structure, hyperthin, but with green mist
suggestions of leaves—As usual, I would
write to you: my alphabet's that same
green, vaguely jade but not so solid
     but of course
I may be the Fat Lady, myself
soon, I keep turning
     into my own creation, a piece
     sculpted of red clay
fat thighs now and heavy shoulders
thumbed out of earth, the lines
     bulked, but
curving, in supplication.

     I also consider sending
     clippings—murder
and the latest on-going suicide—among
our old friends, everything's toothed or
     somehow acid. Azaleas, I hear
bloom in our favorite garden.
     I send a question instead.
     No. A warning, rather:
Do not come here this next April
unless you are quite ready
for my touch.

Old Post Card, with Jotting, of J.
at the Qui-Si-Sana Hotel Coffee Shop

Green Cove Springs, Florida

       Bright morning, one of clarity. Clean air
even with smells of grits and bacon, coffee and
how we puzzled over the word "Quiddity," deciding
it had something to do with a sense of essences—
"One admires Ms. Bishop's 'quiddity,'" that came up
and "up," too, as a verb: the dog jogs by, his bannered
tail "upped" with arrogance. . . a *quid pro quo* for you.
                         Across the road
a barber buzzed a bent neckline, and in the yard
there were mirror shards among the cobbles
where the hotel's boy had watered. Wisteria wrenched
arthritic knuckles on the sill, the sun-gold stucco, and
we were moved to speak of Beauty, but lightly, where
"lightly," and "po-litely" and "quiddity" converged.

What I Can Tell You Is

my skin is soft, still
when I touch it, though
the chins sag down too much—
I can thumb them up
trying to look beguiling—it's just
my eyes blear now, weep too easy.

Allergies, I say, and hope
no one asks to what.

Her Explanation

This rat's scrabble is
because I can't write letters now
to Jonah in Raiford Prison:
he has died.

The habit's hard to break.
I'd write, I'd scribble pages
thinking, can he read all this?
and half apologize
for my good life.

Little things I would describe—
honeysuckle on the fence, or
how the fig tree shriveled up
in summer's blight. He'd answer
by post card, how he missed
                    sunshine.
One time, a line to say
the censor laughed, surprised
an ex-wife'd take such time to write—
        implying caution, and
  don't forget the censor's eyes.

I wrote him how it was in Mexico
and how it looked there; how I
sold a manuscript he'd known—
another post card from him,
"I'm glad to know the poems go well."
(for one who raged at falsehood
he often lied.) I'd like
nothing better than to address
this one to Jonah, wherever
and, self-censored
not apologize.

The truth is
if he had to kill someone
I'm grateful, it was
his second wife.

Of Junk, Treasures

Staurday Started Early: 2:11 a.m.

What you really need is a fire.
—My Father

amid my collection of junk
insatiable, from the stiff pillows
conceiving these cold letters, messages
        I'll never send. . .
here is (gilt framed) my grandmother's
pink watercolor of poppies
and my other grandmother's wool-worked robin—
      yellow-breasted, with black fuzz legs—
not to mention plastic orange daisies
pronged into a Coke bottle
old gift of love from long ago, a birthday
and other echoes (from last night)
"Everybody ought to have a *Guernica*."
            The air moves as if
ten thousand other creations hovered, sly
ready to slip in at the inched open window
or boil, seething down to raw colors
pale poppy pink, plastic orange
        or yellow, wool-threaded
not to mention tons of paper
all that ink.
            This house will explode
someday, a violence of words
and images, burst open.
"A *Guernica* is all I need."
and other lies.

Zones and Circles, Love

Let's start where it began, this morning
with today's weather in the paper, the states
mapped on cheap newsprint, much reduced—

graphic black on white, showing boles or rings
as if the country were a cross-cut tree—isobars
marking our pressures, zone by zone

with time's passage over city, state and peninsula
shown sharp as shadows. It's one long view—
an easy diagram, with few particulars

Items: out the window, today's sky blue
with mid-summer brightness, damp morning
the raintrees' yellow cusped blooms poke into;

a sensual ant's at work there, clawing his hole
deep into sap-vein; here's a nail, hammered
slantwise into the bark. Let's celebrate them, a task

worthy of lust. It's a retrieval, listing and marking
like the map makers' loops and spirals, paisley
patterns tending to oval—an accounting
                as of candles' touch—

the almanac of the anonymous birthdays reached.
And it's trivial, wisp-stitchings of smoke
I list too much. It's an awesome habit. Angels

and alligators and all the "a" creatures. . .
Don't start with that. Stick to morning activities like
the toilet overrunning, or how resolutely

we didn't clean the attic. And all those lurking gifts.
Haven't I warned you, often enough? Those boxes
just wait there, ready to unleash a drowning—

old stuff. A Christmas card turns up
TO MY DARLING DAUGHTER—otherwise it's
mostly trash. I could hear her, quite clearly

saying "don't keep all this stuff forever," but
some of it's from her attic, found
old checks, cancelled, a thank you letter

from someone she charmed at dinner, once.
More items, skillions, for the ubiquitous list.
                    Consider the country's zones
and how many attics left by how many mothers—

And do they watch as we sift through the dust?
Dad suggests, I should hold a burning—
student papers, I know this writing—Her B+

never picked up, so kept. "Do more research."
O, yes. Here are those sandals, sloppy
the grass, and that golf course we walked in sun

saying hello again to the light of day, missing
(who listens to mother?) how the light shown
arm in arm, couldn't of course, be thrown away

reflected in the tiny dew beads, tiny suns
and rainbows. That's a thirst too, summed up.
Here's a Picasso post card. Look again, hello, yes

pubic hair in smudges, and a dance of satyrs
awkward penis, a study of erogenous zones—
the dancers' circles, celebrating that old fart, Death.

O yes. The ant waves
gaily from his hollow, and Death comes by to snip
the taproots, slicing with his swift scissors
whole states clean out of my map.

Let's start again, perhaps with tomorrow's paper—
and a shift in the weather threads. My friend
C, the Pragmatist, says "A zone is a place
        we travel to."

And I say again, "O, yes."

Directive: Do Not Go To Batavia

    Notes from folks who have died collect
in odd corners, Christmas cards from my mother and
directions for getting to Steuben County, the farm
that hasn't been ours for years, and the O you know
reunion places we sometimes visit, as if the past
still lived there, in bits and pieces; there's (I'm sure)
a note from Aunt Bea about going through Victor, and she's
insistent. This was before she was so ill and all—
                                  still going on.

She wrote it big so I'd not mistake the turn off the
turnpike: DO NOT GO TO BATAVIA. I had no intention
of going there, or even to Steuben County—

              death throes of a cockroach interrupted
rattling in old class notes. Bug spray spots the parchment.
Here's the name of a weed I liked, silver in sunlight
in Kansas, a thread-thin white, wheat-like bloom
with a brown dying cockroach kicking its legs—
on his back now, he tenses the middle set like a violinist
cocking his elbow for high C. Silent. Death in the papers.
Batavia, where I never visited, a dream and a Kansas scrawl
saved, for the deaths when a need for poems and names
  crops up.

Waiting for the Dempsey Dumpster Man

*As for wanting to find in all this a broader and loftier
meaning to take home . . . together with the program
and the ice-cream stick, I cannot see the point in
doing so.*
>   —Samuel Beckett, letter to Michel Polac*

notions about drama and verse came along with glimpses into
some backstage world where the Cross-dresser and the clown
ooops. What a flower we found in the upsy-daisy—it grew in
that oldest Garden, wild and silly. It was bent like the back of
Grandfather Time, it was wilted, and ever so smelly. O, daisy
odiferous. "The bowler hats for instance," something glimpsed.
The most human of all emotions is essentially full of smells and
sweats. But I'm no critic. There is no spell-check in my head,
not lately. I dream. I hope. I sniff out garbage scents. A
lovely recipe for growing old: to stumble.

"I do not know who Godot is," he says. Clowns for us. Ice
 cream sticks however, do intrigue me. I want to know why he
thought of that as something to take home and I think keep. All
drama and verse is. Essentially. Like daisies, to be pressed
and programmed but then there's no soul, no daisy freshness,
you see. Kept. It's gone. Just a dryness a shape and a wooden-
ness like O dear. Memories.

*in the *New Yorker*, June 24-July 1, 1996, p. 136. Translation by
    Edith Fournier.

Buying a New Mattress Involves

another letting go, and everything else from the carpet up—
even without considering new paint for the walls, but
incredible feats of the vacuum's suck:
     inspiration of years of dog hair, and dust.

There's inordinate fuss.
There's ridiculous preparation: moving Rodney's bust
and all the volumes of Faulkner, Proust and Stevens, not
     to mention piles of laundry, a miscegenation

of silk scarf and cotton sock; just
making the final, unspeakable decision
when the body's condition is too painful to ignore, is tough.
     And old coils don't support enough.

The mattress, when finally given up
heaves up its ghosts—hardly countless—but
several departed lovers, lost in a breathless groan, like lust
     not quite forgotten, and leaves the house

in a pother—much more turmoil
than made by the old dog, Lola, who went off, not quite
gaily with the vet's man, but giving him her smile
     a small wag of recognition.

Old Ties, for the Asking

For my cousin Debbie, after family reunion

home now, considering cleaning the attic, suitcases
to carry up, and I know what's needed
like Daddy said, is a fire

    stuff left behind, like old ties—

one I think of with bees worked in, the threads
piled in layers, tight gold, to resemble tiny bodies
and plied, loose, for wings—
there's a green crow on another, insolent
so green with age, it's black now
where its neck bends

    to touch it brings visions—

conjures gone parties, jazz riffs, those friends
who wouldn't leave when they ought
and didn't return, when wanted

    it's a rare wonder

how you understood, lately
about that trunk full of photos, my mother's
tin trunk, those strangers' faces I can't throw away

how you said, so gravely, "They need
someone to care," over the red hots, with rain
threatening: these and the other leftovers, I'll save.

Reading, Nightly

How Gulley Jimson's Adam Isn't Mine

A sweet line. I fell for that line. . . . bring his arm right out and have
Eve pushing it away.   [And] make the serpent fatter—fatter than Adam.

—Gulley Jimson, in Joyce Cary's *The Horse's Mouth*

How I was only joking, joshing, making a fake world with iron
  letters
brushed rubric red for their unsaintly seeds, a thirst for apples and
that was me I called Eve in that fable I'd constructed all as if
  brushed—
that's a blush red where she's complaining of too many apples, even
those in my kitchen pulled in, peeled sliced and parboiled those
descendents from the first, Solomon called for when sick of love.
Comfort me with cinnamon, or cloves for love's sake, black rosettes
pricked in a bitter pomander, after he (known only to me as Adam)
has gone. And I hadn't remembered for years 'til this book, as if
it was my mural palimpsest figured on Gulley's blue Adam with
knobbled knees and a wrenched arm his Eve shoved aside. Well
as one of my Grandmothers used to say, exasperated, I never.

That, of course was my mistake. O, easy to say how the world's
an apple, hung in a dark closet and Eden's a lost landscape
somewhere east, with orchards and a brook that snakes, bees
fumbling in marigolds, and laughter's the gift that came later,
  with
tears' release. How in the gone world, gone rotten there's love,
  still
back with a rush, brought back with the scent in the image
  and ink.

Ruth Moon Kempher—33

Thursday Night's Poem

Tomorrow is my day to read all day in Spanish
Mañana, and the days slip by. . .
the old dog ages, kept alive on aspirin
          and love
stands, back knees bent for balance
or a leap to Heaven, her blind eyes showing
         too many whys.

Tomorrow is my day to study Spanish
mañana, Spanish is the loving tongue. . .
and I remember how his shirt felt
        but not his lips
   yes, lips
but more, warm fabric.

The old dog has no appetite, and the young one
slavers after
hound dog days.

Tomorrow is my day for Spanish.
el Quijote, has too many words, he said. . .
Mañana, and then after say, the moon rises—

    an old dog can't tell night from day
    so we walk the beach all hours
        me leading
    the seeing eye, dreaming
in bad Spanish, leading her into gorse

the dune brush—

te quiero, the Spanish
make no distinction, much
between lust and love. The lucid Spanish
say I will be yours, God willing

tomorrow, or some day.

The Kohler Ad

This is a poem: I know it, feel it in my bones—
it's all about death and rumor.
A youth, enamored, plunged to his death
(he'd heard his beautiful girl had died—
untrue). He galloped his horse off an escarpment
where rocks stuck up especially sharp
and where he bled, up sprang tulips—
all this I read
in an ad for a bathroom sink.

The bowl is lovely with tulips. I wish
I could afford to redo my bathroom, in reds
instead of yellows. The ad adds, further. . .
"A tulip offered by a young man to his beloved says
'As the redness of this flower, I am
on fire with love.'"
            And two tulips, cut
lie at the corner of the tilted bowl
whose porcelain blossoms droop coyly—O
I think, no one would dare throw up
into such beauty, or spit toothpaste, flush
        into that golden hole.
Am I grown old?

My beloved has had trouble with his teeth.
I know this: he told me.
Would he set his teeth at the edge of this sink
and gum my shoulder? Is his death
pray God, only rumor?

        I have never
liked questions in poems. Especially

---

questions without answers. I'd almost rather
imagine that youth. His horse bled too, I suppose
mangled, became hyacinths, perhaps, peonies

   bigger and more blowsy than usual—

if I could touch
that sink, it would be cool as my love's fingers—
those tulips, soft as his most private places—
This is my red blood, firing my blush.
It is not an advertisement: it is only a poem
but as such, mirrors more than portraits
awkward, attempts more than I
dare, with my brush.

Cycle for J. Miro, Who Wrote
The Titles [1939-1941]*

1.

"Pink Dusk Fondles the Sex of Women and Birds"

I will write these small lines
for Joan Miro, who merely jotted them down in his journal
clearly labeled "Poem Titles"—and then
off he went.
Maybe the subject was too much.
Nonplussed, perhaps because he was a man, never
wrote a word—
but I can. I know that *frisson*
of color. I, woman, can attest to having seen
ah, my Lord, such pink reflections in car hoods and puddles
giggling tickled (like touching a Chagall peach)
skin tones, with stubble—that blush.
Caught up in impossible situations of closeness
O right. At dusk. And have—speaking of poems—heard
in the background, hens and robins twitter with love.

2.

"The Beautiful Bird Revealing the Unknown to a Pair of Lovers"

Towards the end of Joan Miro's list there are mirror-images.
Reflections of birds. There were the generic flutterers
touched by pink sunset. Then, vaguely, a bird implicit
in *"Drop of Dew Falling from a Bird's Wing"* a lovely
glittering circle which *"Wakens Rosalie Sleeping
in the Shadow of a Spider's Web"* a visible Rosalie
with an exhausted lover, naked beneath web lines, loops
and nooses—he's out of the picture. Excuse me. The poem.

A spun trap for the eye. Very quiet. No music.
And what is *Unknown* that the Beautiful Bird reveals
may be a farcical artist, peeping in the bushes.
Ah, listen! the bird blows the whistle on his espionage:
and it's not the Secrets of the Universe, after all.

3.

"Ciphers and Constellations in Love with a Woman"

This is so circuitous a title it swims:
creates a vision only possible underwater. O on O, in language
particular. A. Woman. I think feminine *la femme. une femme.*
une demoiselle   a wife?   An undersea siren.
This is no woman who chases chickens and sweeps the yard.
This is woman, naked, bathing by tumbling waters, caressed
by long drools of bubble as she dives, curving her fingers
against the liquid blue iridescence and bubbles O on O O
babbling. Diatoms and sand crystals, self-sufficient
  constellations
displaced by her plunge, drift upwards as small suns, aglow
                O on O, streaming away
from her slick hips, her thighs, slithering eel ribbons, upwards.

        She dreams herself a gaunt addict driven—
this figure, that figure—this woman in the abyss, becomes
all women, nature.   nameless.   a cipher herself in
  eclipse.

---

* Joan Miro, *Selected Writings and Interviews,* ed. Margit Rowell, Thames
& Hudson, London, 1986. p. 170.

"Mere Color,"

Jorge Borges reportedly sniffed, on being read
Wallace Stevens' "Sea Surface Full of Clouds"*

                            a bleak dismissal, who
heard
Brilliant iris on the glistening blue, and thought
perhaps too closely, whose
eyes opaque, or closed while listening—
heard *breakfast jelly yellow* streak the poet's deck
as an impinging rudeness . . . *green*
Gave suavity to the perplexed machine
in a pistache of repetitious chocolates
and umbrellas—
. . .*green blooms turning crisped the motley hue*
To clearing opalescence, and wondered
blinded, how.

* Quoted by Willis Barnstone, in *With Borges on an Ordinary Evening
in Buenos Aires: A Memoir*, Urbana: University of Illinois Press, 1993,
p. 176. The quoted lines within my poem are from Wallace Stevens,
"Sea Surface Full of Clouds," *The Collected Poems of Wallace Stevens*,
New York, NY: Alfred A Knopf, 1989, pp. 98-102.

Of Trees—With D. H. L. and Tennessee
in Cohoma County, Mississippi

Evil, what is evil?
There is only one evil, to deny life
   —D. H. Lawrence, "Cypresses"

1.

In the warmth born at midnight
from work put off—trying to remember "Cypresses"
in that balance between waking and sleeping, the past day
and the coming dawn—it's a swelter
of mixed memory: "Cedars of Lebanon" rose up
maybe from dinner at the Lebanese restaurant, friendly heat
   as ice shrank and the glasses trembled
under the host's framed family tree—
squiggles: the Arabic names like curled leaves
and the inked branches sinister, like
evil fingers, grasping

2.

fresh-lit cigarette smoke adrift
(here it's legal) mingled sweet old memories—
we're in from Memphis, where Tennessee
said the Delta begins in the Peabody Hotel lobby—
evocations: a smattering of ducks—
kin of the Peabody's waddlers
seen in an orchard of distorted trees, twisted pecans
deformed by an old year's ice storms, Kenneth told us
as we drove by yesterday and last night, his voice
reciting from Nonno's poem: "beings of a golden kind"
(we saw some, maples and beeches in sunlight at Moon Lake)
"Whose native green must arch above

The earth's. . ." what was it?
"The earth's obscene, corrupting love."*
smiling, eating something Greek, garlic
with mint. . . O mercy. Lebanese.

3.

Sunbuttered leaves, too multi-layered and fluttery
to number, phantom ducks—I carry a cane
with a golden duck-head, that came from New Orleans—
lucky, lost my sunglasses in a different lobby
but a dusky man retrieved them—
Of such ephemora comes heat, this sweat of conscience
the undone work engenders, that task of trapping
        today's bits and pieces
measured against past losses, a heat like that
of the growing green kudzu, as it's
smothering the pines.

* The quoted lines are from Tennessee Williams, *The Night of
the Iguana*, Act III.

Of (Other) Trees, and Weathering

The Hybridizer Crows

Lo, improving ages wait ye! In the orchard of the
  bones. . .
Out with lent! Clap hands postilium! Fastintide is by.
> —James Joyce, *Finnegan's Wake*

and O, it's such an orchard, where fool appleblossoms babble
Did it, Did it. (Listen, rather than explanations, just feel.)
In a bumble of balloons poised from bulbs of barberpoles, O
surprise! Caught those big eyes frankly looking—splat, like
a donkey banged with a slat to catch his attention— I declare
ice cream for all, tutti-fruiti, and tons of it. Pink confetti

Ice cream, I say, with empirical fervor, that improbable
elixir flavor of the Emperor's concupiscent curds. O, yes.
It's a taste of Stevens, timelost in Joyce's world; but let's not
play games. No cruises into nether climes with pop-up daisies
or the patina of flatulent petunias. No spin the bottle. No bingo.
There was a moment of notice, and now there is this orchard

to which I lay my claim. There was no blare of trumpets, nor
ice cream to cool one's fever: those were mere semantic figures
and, of balloons, in fact, a lax elastic on one finger snapped.
But O, surprise, to catch those big eyes looking—O, stars
and galloping garters and grinning angels in the trees. . .
the rest was a whirl of garble and the cider scent of leaves.

Northeast Winds: Of Separation

1.

The first northeaster poem was a night poem—
the wind blew it up like sea skuzz
                    over the dunes—
because I was missing the old dog, somehow
maybe the way the water moved, the surf
slithering four ways at once—she'd have fished
for the silver fish, flick-tail, splashing
her nose in bubbles, no matter.
                    She's close enough
under the dunes, taking a rest
as a good dog should, and the pup was there
beside me, grumbling, toting his piece of wood—
a gentle night that was, if lonesome
with full sea sounds and a full moon sailing
riding an oil-slick, pooled, of cloud.

2.

            Some days, though
it's not so easy, writing. The work takes you
back into sea skuzz, old manuscript dust—
erasures and palimpsests to fumble. That self
supposedly older and wiser, is simply older
meeting up with lost dogs, mirror-image
lovers—it's a homespun curse.
            When the wind blows
northeast, what repeats in pine boughs
and sloughs in the dry palmettos
is sea sound, is greed and a reaching lust—
to dial that number, with old trembles
to say that name again.

Three For My Dad, at 97

> I could see you knew
> what sort of carpentry
> you were.
> —Duane Ackerson, "Weathering"

At Bowling, Monday Night

our League President's wife, Luanne
stopped and leaned by my locker, to say
rather abruptly, "O, hey
I saw the ambulance and the fire truck Thursday—
all those Rescue people at your gate."
   (They live on down my road, Luanne
and the guy she calls her "hubby") So I said—
not so abrupt, but still slow
because I was tired, "That was for
my father." They know
my Dad's ninety-seven, so maybe
it's not so unusual. And I wondered
sort of hopeful, if they'd witnessed his exit—
sitting up erect on his stretcher, fully clothed
   looking for all the world, like
Captain Queeg on his quarterdeck
contemplating some fool's
courts-martial.

At 97, My Dad

lives next door, beside the brown creek
in a trailer he's rebuilt until
it's stronger now, than
when it was new—
repaints the deck he added on back then
every April, so it gleams, fresh-done
after winter—
unwraps the dwarf Australian pine
he's kept from the late frosts
and folds its blanket
for next year
careful, neatly—
keeps his tools neat, too.
Soft-spoken always
when young, played winning tennis
and went to war tall, straight
to do battle with death—
now shuffles a bit, using the walker—
    those replacement hips
but keeps the peace between kids, dogs
and grandkids, my nephew, nieces
listens to us, careful
when he wants to, likes company
good beer, talk of the farm, the latest
books he's read, tennis on television—
knows precisely how
to tune us out.

At Scrabble, One Night

in my Dad's shipshape kitchen, his table cover
bright vinyl, with pears and apples
reminded me (though I was winning at the time)
            of the oilcloth yellow at Gramma's.
He was thinking. Words. He was born ninety-seven
years ago in Upstate New York, and has always—
far as I know—played to win.
            Potatoes. We were talking about
potatoes, for some unknown reason.
He said "Our cellar was always full of potatoes.
If you could keep them longer than anybody, you'd
            get more at market, later."
He's not above creating a tactical diversion, I know
so I waited for his move. Only a few letters left to use.
"When we'd pull potatoes, those days . . . ."
            He put down almost all his tiles
taking exactly the squares I'd meant to use. But I had
two possibilities, and was ready, put down
            whatever word, and he went on

"The horses pulled the harvester, and we'd follow
the plowed lines, pulling potatoes from the dirt—
            me and my grandfather—"
He nodded, seeing my surprise. "I was maybe
eleven then. He was quiet man. He had a tool house.
He was careful of his tools. But I could never beat him
at pulling potatoes, no matter how I tried."
            (I was busy thinking Great-
Grandfather, not Grampa) and he put his last tile—
the blank tile I'd forgotten— on a double score
"That's an X," he said, "Xi, a Greek letter," and won.

Picking Up Things

This morning presents vivid
images of fingers—"Keep in touch"
my mother's phrase—as dense
potted aloes by the open window
raise long, green members
tap the humid air, or curl
into the curtain—
serrate, sensate.

The book I picked has a slick
green cover. Hefting it, I decide
it's a good book; I'm attracted
to ephemera, the ink blush
invisible on my hand.
Mother again—
      "Where'd you get
such weighty notions?"

Fingering ideas, how to touch
some sense of contact, I say
"palpable," and "concrete"—
so proud to make
distinctions
the aloes have forgotten.

"Keep this in mind."
And, of touch—
my mother's hands were always
distant, gloved, in motion
directing a show without puppets
    or, puppets, with no strings.

Subtle as ever—"Mind now"
I don't remember
her buttoning me into
everything.

The Purist of Pear Trees

            this brown moth, fuzz-winged
as if dipped in powdered cocoa, visits my table—
folding his small tent under the news
he lurks, aquiver.
            He comes to remind me of the real world
beyond the windows, as if the book I'm reading—
  Stanley Kunitz
about his gardens—weren't enough, and the papers
from stale morning hadn't warned me:
                        You will meet an old friend.
                        You will enjoy reminiscing.
and a butterfly, earlier in porched pansies
flapped orange into lavender petals. A freeze warning
darkens the air. I know my old pear tree, foolish
                        pushes obstinate buds out
                        old leather
and under my hand, words.

            Here's my old friend:
his pear tree poem. Once, up in Worcester
a bus full of Elizabeth Bishop buffs
were held up by their driver
reading to them: "You'll be seeing
                        this same tree his mother planted."
Rough voiced, the driver a pseudo-Barrymore in mufti
needed Ethel's vibrato:
                        'Make room
                        for the roots.' my mother cries.
                                'Dig the hole deeper.'
We had chocolate-chip cookies in the parlor;
sipped polite lemonade. Finally
were released to the garden
where, leaves buttered yellow by sun, that pear tree
  flourished—

---

mine's dwarfed beside it—great branches uplifted
and in the fork of one, a white ceramic angel
stuck in, lopsided.
                        It was my mother's voice then
                        from the shade—*"Listen.*
                        You come from good roots.
                        You have excellent blood.
                        Don't be afraid."

Mimosa Trees: A Thank-You

Once upon a wayback time, sick still
but swaddled in blankets, I sat
       dreaming death in the air—
radio lists from the War, fronts
where my Dad might be, my friend
Karl's lists of what could kill you—
       milkweed juice, the lumps
in bacon, a drop too much ether—
under a tree with puff blossoms.
It seemed to me, if you tried to hold
those incredible pink blossoms—
       they would, like beautiful
dreams, wither at your touch; held
close, shrivel forever.
           But then
in a later wayback time, I planted
an early mimosa, in earth of my own—
and for many springs, it gifted me
those fuzz flowers, until fronts—
weather fronts—Hurricane X or Z
       hurtled pines; split my tree
to its roots. I grieved. I admit it. Only
the deaths of dogs and a few people
have touched me like that tree's.
       But here's an unlikely hero
and magic, like a dream of survival
blossoms this spring reached
higher than ever, puffs soared
from a tree roped together, shipwise
       by my brother-in-law—
a boat-builder by trade, bowlines
or halyards, or sheets, rigging—
those old arthritic branches flew
       blossoms
as ever, soft pink; golden
pollen dusts earth again.

Of Bees

This could easily drift
into mawkish, comic business, but bees
have been known to inspire dread: my dad
allergic to bee-sting—he fainted
bitten by a honey bumbler—
        and bees
of feeling, my husband's touch, once—
regretted later. Putting bees into words
then, like e-mail—incomprehensible
        as all today's
electronic emissions, zapped notice
for a friend's memorial, or the odd
offhand reference to Uncle Frank
who retired to Florida—yes
for the health of his bees—
delicate to speak of. . . .
        It's hard enough to walk away
remembering fallen heroes, to limp
regretful paths lined with blowsy roses
or jasmine, when the air's alive
        with bees.

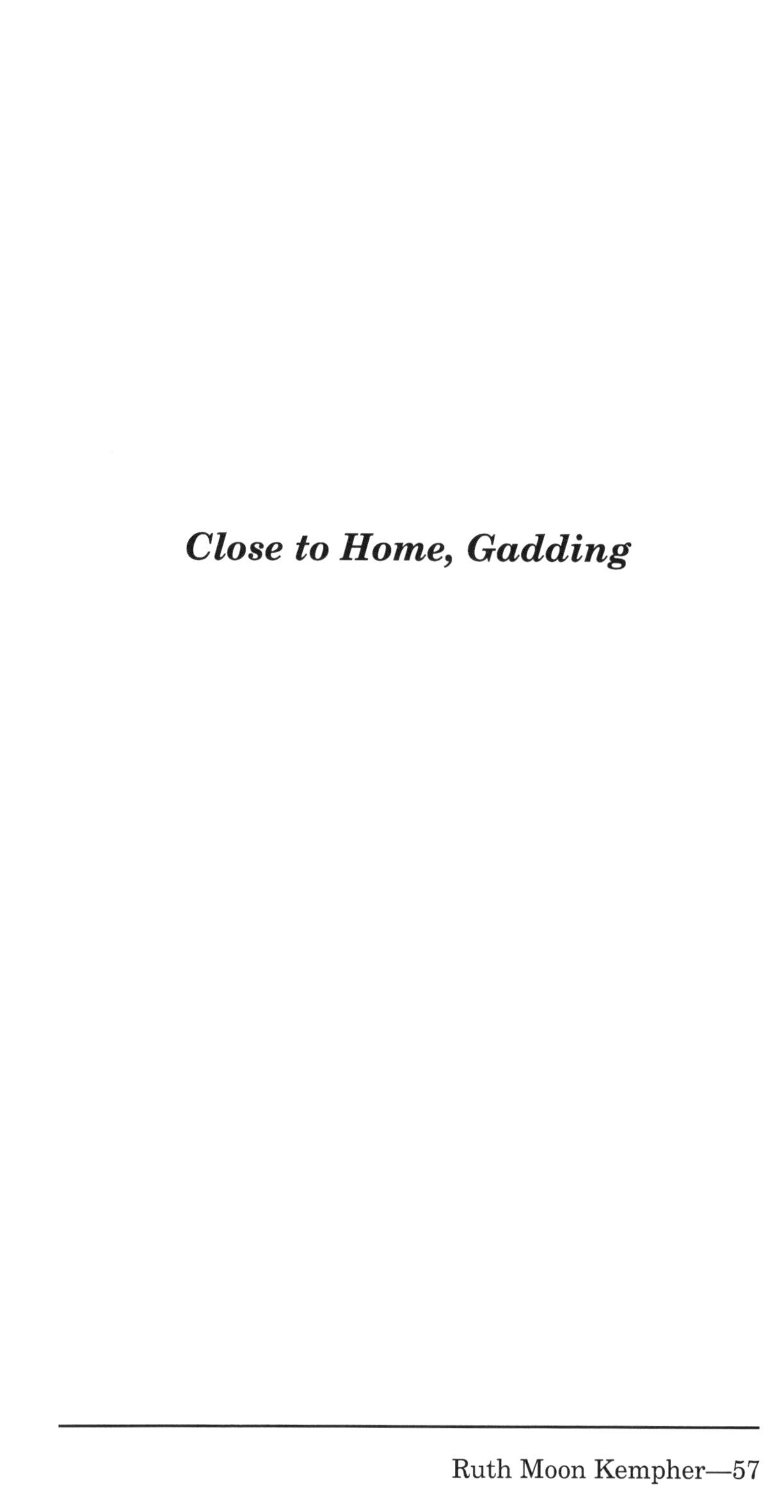

Close to Home, Gadding

Local Gallery

1. **The Lovers**—A Painting by Remedios Varo

She does not paint time, but moments when
time is resting.
—Octavio Paz, "Remedios Varo's
Appearances and Disappearances"

To make a start with actuals, this construct is a
long, tall canvas or rather bristol board, its colors of
"mixed media" predominantly darks: plums, blues,
greys; its lights confined, constrained in a white haze
escaping to rise upward from the central figures, a pair
of

Lovers

long, emaciated bodies
they sit together on a bench
her sag of breasts   his long, tight jacket
highlighted   bright buttons
their hands barely touch
below
(at the center of the nightmare)
their heads, which are gold-rimmed mirrors
her eyes reflect a glance   his eyes repeat, oblique
caught here, guilty.
They've generated so much emotion
that vapors rise, white, from behind their shoulders
becoming light clouds that drift up, up to the
topmost framing
where drops form, drops that fall down, dripping
to the framework's bottom
where waves are swept by unseen currents
already subsuming the lovers' feet—
a dark flood, rising. They will drown
soon, lost in their dream.

---

2. Nostalgia: Clayton Powers' Painting
                 "Shrimp Boats at Salvador's Dock"

There's heat in the oils of this painting—
the heat waves, in the way he laid his palette knife to make
                the white oak planking of the hulls
                two shrimp boats drifting
                and the verdigris / mildew of the dock

Heat peels in the cypress board facade of Salvador's Fish
  Market
now vanished, but still carefully here, the shop
                where I bought shrimp long ago. Bait.
                A man with grizzled jaws leered
                leaning on the counter.

He scared me. I know too much about this painting:
too much about the artist who tended bar at the
  Tradewinds
                drank margueritas with his first wife
                Clementine, white-haired lovely
                a classy lady

I bowled with his second wife, Harlene, who left town
lately, with their daughter.
                Heat flakes off, like rust
                from taut, brushed-in chains of anchors
                unseen, underwater, rippled water
      reflecting sky
                as I remember Clayton

who played the gut-bucket at the old Tradewinds
fell off one night, broke his wrist
                and went out painting, arm in a sling

to this place where heat survives
no matter who feels it—
heat, alive.

3. **Portrait Untitled**

One of
the un-
finished pictures
Jonah left is of this
woman
open-kneed &
barstooled with her skirt
hiked up to show
almost something: elbows
green skin somehow obscene
& at the same time
fertile.

When I asked him
who is this woman?
he in his sometimes
pompous way said, O
she's just a slut I saw
in the Pennsy Station bar
but the older I grow
& the more
poems there are—
ink fresh black semen
the more
she looks (of course)
like me.

4. Arabesque—After Lorca's Drawing:
"Marinero borracho," ("Drunken Sailor") 1934

tipsy-turvy, it's yes indeedy a double vision a before and
after turning, as if a performance of ballet moves, sinuous
two sailors, one sober seen on the left, sinistrally sober
outdoors under a crescent moon seen possibly as an omen
of feminine influence. Well. Maybe. Same sailor now seen
inside O he's gone into the tavern no longer standing but
seated, a table and a bottle labeled *ROM* in his fingers O
his fingernails are gone and so is his neck hair. O dear.
Talk about transformations. Four dotted lines run up his
collar as roadways for a word shift from *ROM* to *AMOR*
in the general direction of his heart. The poet's word of
course, that's straight and clear but the lines do a sudden
up twist, a Rococo curve up into *ROMA*, a destination
fraught with fear, or anguish, or both, tip-toeing around
what I like most, how his cap ribbons, at first so lively
and perked upwards now droop like moist fettuccini, here.

5. Drawing Lesson: Balloons

> Essentials include a knack
> for shading, the side of the pencil
> shaved just so, angled
>
> but O, the spaces
> left white express the sensual ovals
> void of all but air, made solid, elongate—
>
> that's the business of line, a visual
> thinness of taut rubber and what's most
> important, erased.

History, They Want, Contemporary

comment /   conservation and topical
and my exuberant excess of lust's

o rats, hysterical   and there's no
understanding of / touch of love's

they want Pissarro and Ponce now
and how the town was built of

like the three little pigs / straw
twigs and bricks / they want ecolo

gy they want how it rained fish
in a terrible thunder / they want

pollution on the beaches, which
only reminds me again and again

how sand is, under the shoulders
how weights fit against each

but this is not what they want
these ragtag treasures / hot

and this poem is not either
what they want.

Of the Rain's Songs—

At the Tradewinds Lounge, Charlotte Street

1.

Begin with new shoes. White sandals
nestled in crumpled tissue. A turpentine, or oily odor as if
painted leather. Artistry of difference
                    in a box labeled *Capezio*:
    Cobbler to Dance People, Fashion People
a poem in progress
          tickled me, pink paper
      visions of Sprung Rhythm—always inept
      out of date as the Romantics—
        a music musing with steps and paces
a ghost waltz in this wet weather

sandaled

2.

     moving ahead. Here, Angie the owner
my friend who lets me run a tab, sits, sips
          her margarita, lime odor drifts
    a pungent acid: she's a redhead, one of *Capezio's*
People
      People   reminds me I'm not. Dream too much
      drink scotch and think too much
         hearing drips and nonexistent
    but it was raining again

3.

    where this began, in Atlanta, in rain.
(Of things I think I know, there's always
      the color of rain.) I was mixing colors, that pink

---

of the tissue
         the soft skin of his—but I forget myself
unacceptable. Unfrocked sandals, the priest confessed
             trip and stumble of clumsy
       fingers. Where was I?
    there is no rainbow, he whispered
      unless there's rain. Sing me
        rain songs, insistent

4.

       They have a storm machine here.
Waxy, the bartending candle-maker chuckles
     twirls his thick moustache and
         pours another margarita, punches a button
             twinkletoes, he's
      a villain. Makes rain from buckets
                down plastic gutters—
  it spatters on Angie's shoulders
        watering slick plastic palm fronds
          superfluous. With a crash
    of tin foil thunder, drizzles

5.

I remember white dogwood, tiny leather petals
         curled, pink-ochre-tipped, outside my window
            cupping rain

6.

  Jennie, across from Angie's a *Capezio*
Dance People. Unaware. Her clothes move, loose
              mou-mou, a tube of floral jersey

---

over hidden thighs, expressive, plump. Her mouth
  sensual, behind a pirouette of fingers
      a cigarette she stole from Jim
    her husband: asks me (Jennie) do I notice
     how people live together long enough
          look like
    each other's dog as Waxy
         makes it rain again, crashes
that tin thunder. Jimmy Buffet on the jukebox
  words and music, drowned.

7.

    Carry a crumpled pack of Winstons, myself
  as amulet, crazy. But here it is, another prop
        real as anything else here
  his hands, how he moves the cigarette to his face
    a fluid motion, a screening so well-rehearsed it's
     like an abbreviation, an act of attrition
    listening to how he said rain always
  makes him horny, smiling: Did you really
      look for me all morning
    in the rain

8.

    There's a strawberry appliquéd by Jennie
in the crotch of Jim's denim jeans. I had planned to be
  Clown People in my new sandals by *Capezio*, with a
trick
    clown-bright bent umbrella but
  he found me dreaming, barefoot
     "Remind me," I said, "always, always
        to order rain" Watch now as
  sunshine

---

dapples plastic, in this rain of chlorine green.
Dreaming
          his favorite, dry martini—the exact
          color of the rain.

Commedia Dell'Arte,
Too Late, At the Tradewinds

There was background: some more, some less.
As if we'd dragged as luggage or baggage all those dusty
trappings of the past—smack dab looted the Carnival, the
Circus, even the Operatic, sets for the clown scenes, Fools'
masques and gravediggers' clods. Up to my old tricks,
scene shifting like Uncle Proteus's favorite imp, I'd be-
come the Fat Lady once again, sighing. He was impressed
(the one I always play to) sigh for sigh. "You're not con-
tent with your situation; you have the old grin plastered
on, but I have reservations, how you feel, inside. Not
that I could help, you understand. But I do empathize."
Blinking. Thick eyelashes dripping mascara. "Do I hear
violins? Or is that a yanking on my heartstrings?"

I nodded several pounds of chin. "I tug. I yank.
The old routines are my stock in trade."

Bless him, he did a bit of the soft shoe, to amuse
me. Candles. Let's not forget that candlelight—the fishnet
yellow citronella ones that do in the mosquitoes (small
deaths, all the time) as they glamorize. That was no
violin. An old man was playing an accordion. I do indeed
remember. The roses bloomed up from his hands, opening
out like crystal petals of a fountain, frozen, glittering in
the sun.

Of Key, And Time

and how I am grown old, always the black purse
swallows them and now it's my glasses and where I
was hot natured, sweaty always it's gotten so I'm also
looking for a sweater, or jacket, eyeing that sports two
sleeves hanging at the table: cold is what keys are,
once you can find them that's not much changed,
eyeing someone's empty sleeves dreaming heat of the
absent or negative non-body, can chill a moment quick
as "no," spoken or tacit, looking for clues in the silence.
O it's Saint Me, perfectly smugly sly as a demon
expecting cake and eating double exposures, like
mirror visions, plus and minus: key words. Didn't you
know? Walls of words and silences need those quirked
openers those corkscrewed expressions, country music
sometimes is sung in (key, key, you idiot.)
perseverance. Improper stars. Rain.

The Sidewalk Artist's Legacy

Look for me seaside, in those polyps you'll remember
on crabshells, sharp-edged barnacle uprisings, veined
purple, or better, blood red, sometimes on rocks, under
coiled wet seaweed filaments—watch your foot. Look for
me in the trash of roadside diners, milkweed pods' opaque
ooze, or tiny petaled blue asters, those lines
a scrape of pastel—my blurred self portrait, head and
shoulders in cloud's too simple: look for formal, if
disjointed values, lost in Time's prism, fingering off into
blue. Look for me in white spaces that define
an anemone's corolla, shadowed to catch your look.

Found on Aviles Street:
Fred-Fred

Fred-Fred, the artist's dog's
been trained to snap
at angels. He sleeps on his paws
    warily
just in case.

Oops! Gotcha.

The Health Department complains
when people leave Fred-Fred
old bologna sandwiches
    like casual offerings

but he's unimpressed—
leaves them, hip-haunching away.

They leave sardines.
They leave liverwurst and cheese.
But actually, Fred-Fred's only
partial to Dago Red. And

garbanzo beans. And
angels.

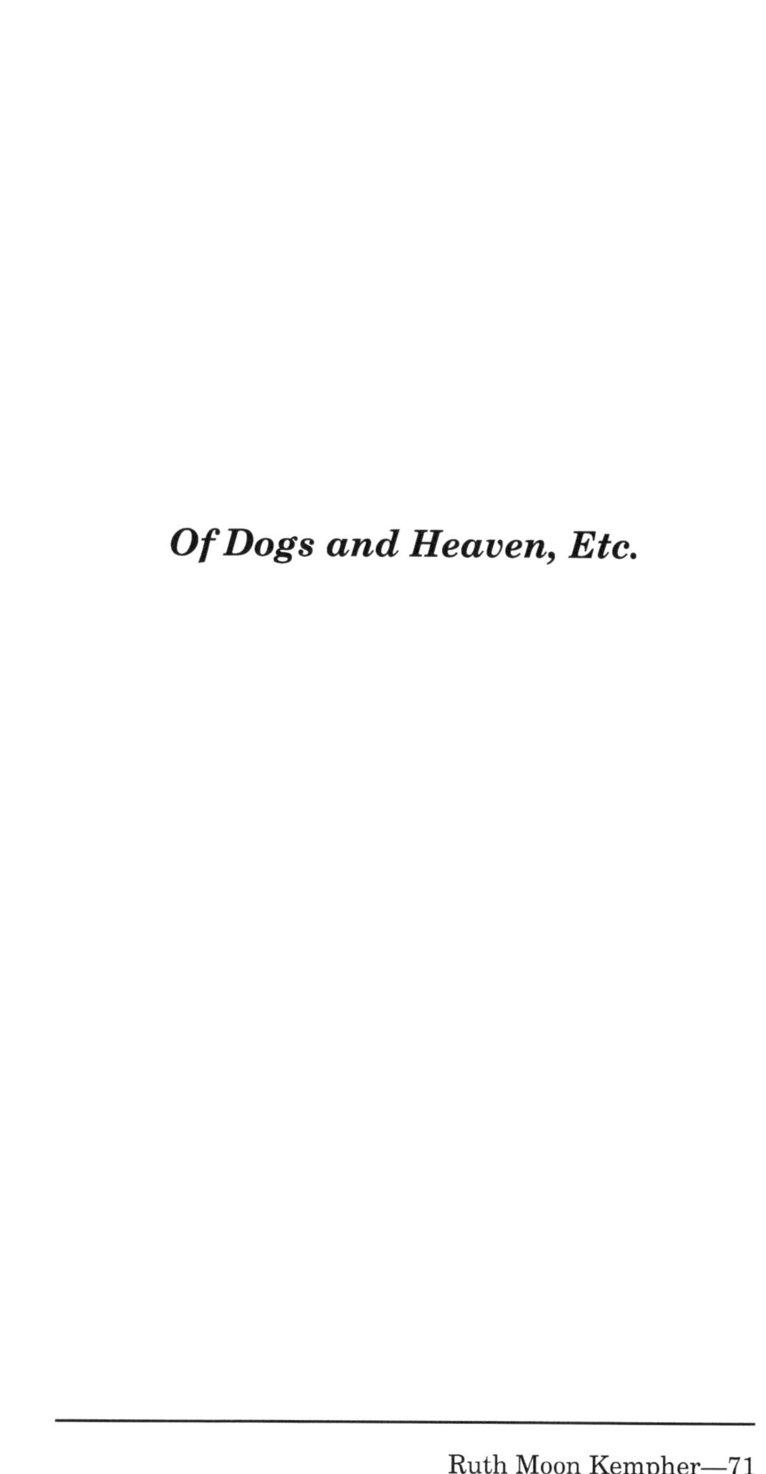

Of Dogs and Heaven, Etc.

How the House Moves
With the Morning

Even the brightest poem is haunted by shadows
Mark Strand, "Shadow"

something starts it, stirs
the gauze and twine web of the curtains

something clicks
beyond the thermostat, as a fan whirrs—
it's that old refrigerator, its age showing—

a small dance of morning, it begins with dogs
out of night's lethargy, prancing on the sofa
denting the cushions, long tongues lolling

or maybe the ashes in the fireplace—
echoes of lost blazes—flare an embered grace.

In a benediction of departure
harsh visions of night vanish, fading away
as sunlight brushes living-room lace—
                              but shadows linger
in the striped-leaved yam plant on the table
tangle, *chiaroscuro*, myriad beginnings
and endings sway together

in the blink of an eye, the walls
move back to place.

If A Dog Bit an Angel

who would know, to tell it
except by the smell? Of course
other dogs would: in their way
saying Hello hindmost
O what's this? just a whiff
sanctified by God, of dinner
or just a snack? a taco? There's
a provisional ukase from Heaven—
we provide for drunks and sinners
madmen, saints and dogs. Maybe
artists, also.
        They are digging up
the cobbles of Aviles Street and
I know what they won't find—
my friend the artist, long deceased
probably no angel, and likewise
his dog Fred-Fred who both
haunt that street for me.
Fred-Fred was trained to bite
angels, snatch them
flap dab just as he'd jump
whoa, up upright. . . .
        Now Sam, my hound
quite unlike Fred-Fred was never
taught to menace a soul—but
he's dreaming—a feather
drifts: Sam smiles.

Florida Suite

I. Dawn

three surfers bunch up, out where water raises its ridg-
es that curl and crumple white surf touched pink by
the rising sun's light—there are porpoise feeding, bang-
ing the surface with their grins—a tang of salt, brine. A
mullet fisher's net blooms explosive in the middle dis-
tance, surprises space and light flaring under blue sky,
its containment shimmers with mute clangor, muffled
cries we hardly hear, I and the old dog, surfside, find-
ing places sand-scoured at a proper tide, green pools
and in sea scum, a heron fishing on one prop of a leg,
the other claw tucked up high—healthy, his hunger for
the lavender crabs danced up, tip-claw as if in all the
centuries of progress nothing changes. Eat or die

II. Mid-day

bees. business. liverworts close up afternoons, balled
up green and a wrong voice on the phone Hello?
Yes. It's nobody's business but maybe in Ocala, where
mermaids gambol or further down roads—do you notice
how city blocks hang down the hillside, patterns of tile,
reeking and of mermaids, billboards show them with
tails more sea horse than fish, pointing west to Crystal
River, home of stout maidenly manatees. Laughing
how some guys love the heft of a heavyweight mistress,
we ate our shrimp with much scotch and gusto on a
porch overrun with trysting secretaries, where on an
island across dark water monkeys hung, waving, like
ganglia in a second-rate dream: good-bye. Leaving the
world going on with one less angel what we didn't know
couldn't hurt us or, not 'til later

III. Moon-Rise

ghost light glow may be spirit of tabasco, or cayenne in
palmettos, where neon lobsters in a window creaking
advise these from Maine are market-priced, an arm
and a leg says my friend from bowling who is never
confused about such things, notes the triple pawn shop
balls over-hanging every other corner— the tuft-eared
owl glides down to guide me, perched on the gate post
pedestal, his wide eyes reflect solar powered lantern
light. He knows, as my dogs know, what I can only
guess at: who's here with us, shadows and whispered
voices under the pines. When I'm home here in the
woods, out with the dogs at moon-rise, the voices rise
just beyond the soughing branches with their surf-
sounds, as the clouds skud by. Some times I'll mis-
take my Dad's for another's but I listen, always. It's a
tradition: after so much loss we went ahead planting
our roots where there's not enough rain, or next day,
a deluge. Other delusion: hiss and scent of fresh can's
coffee promise morning will arrive in time

Looms— A Digression

Home Economics, a class
back in Coronado, left me impressed
with imagery of weaving: the shuttle's
unstopping movement, warp over weft
or was it, woof? the other way, the cloth
that slips off, vari-patterned, gay
with a life of its own. . .

I wanted to construct like that
except I'd use other stuffs, like twigs—
mesquite, maybe, or bird feathers—crazy
started unbending question marks
I'd slip in, twisted rag mornings
coffee-stained, or crumpled
tinfoil, until

last summer. Storms came
and the weatherman's word was
"Looming." Pointer tip on isobars
coiled like fallen phonelines, expectant
county by county, urgent patterns
in paisley loops of leaf and rain.

I already tangle the names.

Failing, I'll use Donna: that lost roof
and eaten dunes, tossed garbage cans, dogs
and me evacuated—old blind Koko and Bacon
the grey hound who leaped downstairs
to kill a rat as we were leaving—that rain
in slashed palmettos. Home economic
crabbed and intricate details.

Moment Apocalyptic: With Bubba,
The German Shepherd, and a Bluefish

Tomorrow, I said, way back, will be another anomaly
but somehow sunnier, when if ever I can finish this
because the aluminum spoon, on plastic scales
                    goes awkward
the scales bend over, fly down to the floor—
fish scales, though I dream a concertina, mellow—
it was supposed to be cool and cloudy, a northeaster
weather like music, a vast poetic concerto
best forgotten. I tell you, Bubba, it's apocalyptic
how I keep mislaying my epigrams, Ferlinghetti
                        all those people
and you don't know an epigram from Jesus, do you?
I'd forgotten how bluefish flesh turns blue again
like surf water under west wind, under the faucet—
the cold water, tapped, flows cold
and the white ribbed fishmeat turns blue-green—
it's an interior rainbow, with peacock feathering
ripples. "Poets are litmus paper." That was it.
Someone said it. "They test the acidity of our days
and the sourness of their generations."
State of my mind: amazed. How the flesh
held under water turns blue-green—live wetness
and the guts are blood brown, pollen yellow.

Tomorrow may bring another mental trauma, Bubba.
Some other half-caught memory slips off the hook.
                    And there that head sits, mauve eyes
filmed for swimming; seeping those life fluids
into yesterday's newsprint—looking out, today.

Journal Entry: November 7

too early for Thanksgiving, and too many deaths
have come, tough blows, out of unforgiving Heaven—
so that any smile that creeps to my lips is an occasion
and a laugh, God knows, a rare blessing. Here's this
table laid out in my dining room . . . pumpkin left
from Halloween when the kids came to dinner
and a drift of papers: invitation to hear the Poet
known here as Spiel read his work out in Pueblo
lists of places to send poems and bits of onion
where the bowl sits with bluefish and bread chunks
and a yellow page with lines from Williams. . .
Tennessee, not William Carlos, but he's underneath
in a stack that tilts perilous, dry parsley and pepper—
ah Lord, it's the wrong season, but I'm grateful—
we will have fish loaf, the dogs and I, and dreams
of a better time, lemon juice scented, but literate.

Of Dogs and Heaven

and other agencies for finding lost or strayed
old lovers, people like Magda's sister who was telling
everyone in hearing distance at Conrad's wedding how
the flood was; how it came in the night, a rush of water
hell-bent or sent; and I wondered about one in particu-
lar, is he alive still, or in some Heaven which because
of his wife I'm sure someday he'll deserve—Magda's
sister in a chiffon sheath like a beige shroud, slyly told
how they moved upriver, thirty years ago, she and her
husband, uprooted to get away from crabby neighbors
next door, and how on the day the boxcars exploded
all the gases gathered over the water and traveled
downstream, and I just went drifting into my own vi-
sion of Heaven, his blueeyes twinkling, always asked
how am I lately and the dogs? polite. But this is not
about him even if he had dachshunds for his kids and
knew. That thought led to the notion there are no dogs
in my mother's Heaven. They're simply not allowed.
Lord knows, she tried to like mine, but was too fastidi-
ous and they sense that. They'd pant and drool and
push to greet her, grinning. Idiots. The Trooper who
rescued Magda's sister asked her how come, didn't she
listen to the TV? Then I considered ex-husband Jonah,
there with my mother and maybe Koko our first good
old hound—Koko, even at eighteen and sort of senile,
understood him better than I did but when she died at
nineteen, and he said I wasn't grieving, I knew then
how little he knew. The Shepherd pup, black Bubba,
staggered up and peed on his shoe. Magda's sister
shifted to telling how her husband paid fifty bucks for
a kilt that was the wrong tartan, while I'd been dream-
ing that miasma moving on the water like Pharaoh's
plague slipping under the door, seeing green fog mov-
ing upwards, and confused I was thinking maybe there
won't be any people in my Heaven, only dogs.

<hr>

Descending Now

into true dream, your arms slide me crosswise
against your heart, so I travel long corridors
of grapple and remember as today submerges.

Here's a forest, deep with trees and fog, always
dark grasses—cobwebs aglitter with someone's
leftover tears—you could sell them at Tiffany's
if they were stiffer.

       I write jokes about guitars for you
and there's hope—a belief in pencils, close to
belief, moves across the page. My strange
poem is a dream, deliberate, where your arms
are hungry, sliding me into music—

if music could be made to, like a movie—
reel backwards, to respool itself in strands
back inside the guitar's hollows
I would be there always, with the fog
in the depths of trees, where you cover me
like a blanket, with your warm

Get-Away (Undated)

In the city
there were magnolias and
jungle gyms you know—
rust in the garden.

They brought me a purse
that once belonged to my mother—
the silver was smudged black
and bits of leather

stuck to a penny
like furze.

In a desk drawer
I found a wooden mushroom
          growing in furls
and flowers
of dust.

I'd have played the piano
          (like Gershwin)
          but
there was so much rain

already making rhythm
down the world.

About The Author

Ruth Moon Kempher, an ex-navy brat who was born in Red Bank, NJ, has had her poetry and short prose—fiction and critical articles—appear in journals and other periodical publications since early verse publications in *The Saturday Evening Post, McCall*'s and *The Village Voice* in the early 1960's, at about the time she first made a home with her husband in St. Augustine, Florida. She is now retired from owning The White Lion Tavern in the historic San Agustin Antigua area, and from teaching—first for Flagler College while attaining her BA, and graduating with the college's first class; and later, after achieving her MA at Emory University in Atlanta, in the English Department of St. Johns River Community College. Since 1994, she has published the work of many poets through her Kings Estate Press, in single chapbooks and anthologies, collections which are always illustrated. For some time, she has traveled extensively in order to research the work of writers who are also artists. After years of living at the beach, she now lives in the woods in an old cracker house, with two dogs, Sadie, a long-legged hound, and Mister Frost, an emotional American Husky.

About the Book

What I Can Tell You was designed by Bertha Rogers. The typeface, set by Lawrence E. Shaw and Marlise Cammer, for the text and cover is Adobe InDesign CS2 New Century Schoolbook. The book was printed on 60-lb. offset, acid-free, recycled paper in the United States of America. This first edition is limited to copies in paper wrapper.

About Bright Hill Press

OUR MISSION: To seek out, study, and collect the work of early and contemporary writers, storytellers, and artists, and to publish, disseminate, and present that work through publications and educational and public programs for the larger community.

OUR HISTORY: Bright Hill Press/Word Thursdays was founded in 1992 by Bertha Rogers, with the assistance of Ernest M. Fishman. A writer, teacher, and visual artist, Ms. Rogers serves as the organization's executive director and editor in chief. Mr. Fishman has served BHP as president and/or chief financial officer since its beginnings. Bright Hill Press is located at Bright Hill Literary Center, 94 Church Street, in the hamlet of Treadwell, in New York's Catskill Mountain Region; program participants are from Delaware, Otsego, Sullivan, Schoharie, Broome, and Chenango counties as well. Programs and services have grown to meet the stated and implied needs of both youth and adult populations in those counties, as well as the needs of the literary community in New York State and beyond. BHP's current administrative focus is on long-range planning, in order to better fulfill its mission and expand its programs.

OUR ARTISTIC PHILOSOPHY: Bright Hill Press is dedicated to increasing audiences' appreciation of the writing arts and oral traditions that comprise American literature, and to encouraging and furthering the tradition of oral poetry and writing in the Catskills. Writers and artists who participate in BHP's programs are selected for their artistic excellence, their ability and willingness to work within a community setting, and the diversity of their backgrounds, genres, and styles. BHP understands that recognition of the need for a literary community and a commitment to lifelong learning are critical aspects of audience development; the organization's programs for children and adults engender the spirit, craft, and imagination that make this possible.

OUR PROGRAMS are offered to people of all ages. Current program offerings include:
- Word Thursdays, a reading series begun in 1992 and presenting open readings followed by readings and discussion by featured authors;
- Bright Hill Books, publishing anthologies as well as poetry collections and chapbooks and interdisciplinary collections by individual authors since 1994;

- New York State's Literary Web Site, nyslittree.org (since 1999), and the New York State Literary Map (in print and online), developed and administered by BHP, in partnership with the New York State Council on the Arts;
- Word Thursdays Share the Words HS Poetry Mentoring Program and Competition, affording young poets a chance to write and present their own poetry in a public competition since 1996;
- Word Thursdays Literary Workshops for Kids & Adults, offering, since 1994, innovative programs that celebrate and incorporate the elegant use of words with other disciplines;
- BHLC Internship Program for College and HS Students, offering, since 1994, students an opportunity to learn the business of literature.
- Bright Hill Presents: Annual History & Nonfiction Day; Chamber music in the library; and Songs from the Great American Songbook

OUR FACILITIES include The Bright Hill Literary Center Complex:
- BHLC Education Wing, a year-round facility for writing and visual arts classes;
- The Word & Image Gallery, dedicated, since 2002, to presenting works by regional and national artists that integrate words and images;
- Bright Hill Library & Internet Wing, since 2004, a facility with more than 15,000 titles of prose and poetry, art, reference, nature, and children's books for the immediate and larger community;
- Patterns Literary Garden & The Secret Garden, an outdoor space for the whole community, landscaped and created by Catskill Outdoor Educational Corps, a program of Americorps at SUNY Delhi;
- The Kitchen Bookstore, with used books of all genres;
- Offices for staff;
- Guest rooms for visiting and in-residency writers and artists.

GOVERNANCE: Bright Hill Press/Word Thursdays is an independent 501 (c) (3), not-for-profit corporation governed by a board of directors representing the community the organization serves, and an advisory board from the larger community.

Bright Hill Press Books

Bright Hill Press
Poetry Book Award Series

What I Can Tell You
Ruth Moon Kempher   2013 $16
2012 Poetry Book Award, Chosen by Philip Mosley

Outside Come In
Ryan J. Browne   2012 $16
2010 Poetry Book Award, Chosen by Neil Shepard

Almond Town
Margaret Young   2011 $16
2009 Poetry Book Award, Chosen by Colette Inez

Raven's Paradise
Red Hawk   2010 $16
2008 Poetry Book Award, Chosen by Rhina Espaillat

Infinite Beginnings
Lucyna Prostko 2009 $16
2007 Poetry Book Award, Chosen by Joan Larkin

How the Brain Grew Back Its Own History
Liz Beasley 2008 $14
2006 Poetry Book Award, Chosen by Jay Rogoff

Need-Fire
Becky Gould Gibson 2007 $14
2005 Poetry Book Award, Chosen by Liz Rosenberg

The Artist As Alice: From a Photographer's Life
Darcy Cummings 2006 $14
2004 Poetry Book Award, Chosen by Carolyne Wright

The Aerialist
Victoria Hallerman 2005 $12
2003 Poetry Book Award. Chosen by Martin Mitchell

Strange Gravity
Lisa Rhoades 2004 $12
2002 Poetry Book Award, Chosen by Elaine Terranova

The Singer's Temple
Barbara Hurd 2003 $12
2001 Poetry Book Award, Chosen by Richard Frost

Heart, with Piano Wire
Richard Deutch 2002 $12
2000 Poetry Book Award, Chosen by Maurice Kenny

My Father & Miro & Other Poems
Claudia M. Reder 2001 $12
1999 Poetry Book Award, Chosen by Colette Inez

Traveling Through Glass
Beth Copeland Vargo 2000 $12
1998 Poetry Book Award, Chosen by Karen Swenson

To Fit Your Heart into the Body
Judith Neeld 1999 $12
1997 Poetry Book Award, Chosen by Richard Foerster

Blue Wolves
Regina O'Melveny 1997 $12
1996 Poetry Book Award, Chosen by Michael Waters

My Own Hundred Doors
Pam Bernard 1996 $10
1996 Poetry Book Award, Chosen by Carol Frost

Bright Hill Press
Poetry Book Series

Orenoque, Wetumka, & Other Poems
Robert Bensen   2012 $18

Flares and Fathoms
Margot Farrington 2005 $14

Every Infant's Blood
Graham Duncan 2002 $14.95

Bright Hill Press At Hand Poetry Chapbook Award Series

Self-Portrait / Sixteen Sevenlings   Rodger Moody   2013 $10
(2012 Poetry Chapbook Award)
A Tide of A Hundred Mountains Richard Levine 2012 $10
(2011 Poetry Chapbook Award)
Counterpoint Jean Hollander   2011 $10
(2010 Poetry Chapbook Award)
The Infatuations and Infidelities of Pronouns
Christopher Bursk   2011 $10
(2009 Poetry Chapbook Award)
Haywire   Rachel Contreni Flynn 2009 $10
(2007 Poetry Chapbook Award)
The Cut Worm   Douglas Korb 2008 $8
(2006 Poetry Chapbook Award)
A Sense of Place Bhikshuni Weisbrot 2007 $8
(2005 Poetry Chapbook Award)
Gobbo: A Solitaire's Opera David Cappella 2006 $8
(2004 Poetry Chapbook Award)
Web-Watching Bruce Bennett 2005 $8
(2003 Poetry Chapbook Award)
Possum Shelby Stephenson 2004 $8
(2002 Poetry Chapbook Award)
First Probe to Antarctica Barry Ballard 2003 $8
(2001 Poetry Chapbook Award)
Inspiration Point Matthew J. Spireng 2002 $8
(2000 Poetry Chapbook Award)
What Falls Away Steve Lautermilch 2001 $8
(1999 Poetry Chapbook Award)
Whatever Was Ripe William Jolliff 1999 $8
(1997 Poetry Chapbook Award)
The Man Who Went Out for Cigarettes
Adrian Blevins 1996 $8 (1995 Poetry Chapbook Award)

Bright Hill Press At Hand Fiction Chapbook Award Series

Low Country Stories   Lisa Harris $8
(1996 Fiction Chapbook Award)
Boxes   Lisa Harris $8
(1998 Fiction Chapbook Award)

Bright Hill Press At Hand Poetry Chapbook Series

Dancing Bears   Karen Fabiane   2011 $10
A Plastic Bag of Red Cells   Annie Petrie-Sauter   2010 $10
Skunk Night Sonnets   Daniel Waters   2009 $10
The Wooden Bowl   Sharon Ruetenik   2009 $10
Love in the End   Mary Kay Rummel   2008 $10
Effects of Sunlight in the Fog   Alan Catlin   2008 $10
Picking Up   Evelyn Duncan   2008 $8
The Lily Poems   Liz Rosenberg   2008 $8
The Courtship and Other Tales   Kathryn Ugoretz   2007 $8
Hairpin Loop   Anne Blonstein   2007 $8
The Coriolis Effect   Michael Dowdy   2007 $8
It Does Not   Julia Suarez   2006 $8
In Late Fields   Steven Ostrowski   2006 $8
Instinct   Joanna Straughn   2006 $8
Autobiography of My Hand   Kurt S. Olsson   2006 $8
Degrees of Freedom   Nicholas Johnson   2006 $8
Walking Back the Cat   Lynn Pattison   2005 $8
The Spirit of the Walrus   ElisaVietta Ritchie   2005 $8
LightsOut   Tom Lavazzi   2005 $8
The Last Best Motif   Naton Leslie   2005 $6

Bright Hill Press Anthologies

Speaking the Words Anthology 1994 $6.95

The Word Thursdays Anthology of Poetry & Fiction
1995 $12.95

The Second Word Thursdays Anthology:
Poetry & Prose by Bright Hill Press Writers
1999 $19.95

Bright Hill Press Word & Image Series

Suddenly There Were Leaves $22
Poetry & Prose by Main View Gallery & Studio Artists
Edited by Bertha Rogers

How Looking Becomes Seeing:
Word Thursdays Youth Workshops Museum Research, Writing,
& Visual Art Program
Edited by Bertha Rogers $20 (forthcoming)

Breathing the Monster Alive
Eric Gansworth 2006 $16

On the Watershed: The Natural World of New York's Catskill
Mountain Region / Poetry & Prose by Catskill Student Writers
Edited by Bertha Rogers 2001 $14.95

Out of the Catskills & Just Beyond
Literary & Visual Works by Catskill Writers & Artists
Edited by Bertha Rogers 1997 $24

Iroquois Voices, Iroquois Visions
A Celebration of Contemporary Six Nations Arts
Edited by Bertha Rogers, with Maurice Kenny,
Tom Huff, & Robert Bensen 1996 $15

Bright Hill Press Exhibition Series

Bright Hill Book Arts 2010 $16
Edited by Bertha Rogers
Curated by Elsi Vassdal Ellis & Bertha Rogers

Bright Hill Book Arts 2008 $16
Edited by Bertha Rogers
Juried by Keith Smith & Bertha Rogers

Bright Hill Book Arts 2007 $16
Edited by Bertha Rogers
With commentary by Karen Hanmer & Bertha Rogers
Bright Hill Book Arts 2006 $16
Edited by Bertha Rogers
With commentary by Richard Minksy & Bertha Rogers

Bright Hill Book Arts 2005 $16
Edited by Bertha Rogers
With commentary by Edward Hutchins & Bertha Rogers

Bright Hill Book Arts 2004 $12
Edited by Bertha Rogers
With commentary by Nancy Callahan & Louise Neaderland
Bright Hill Book Arts 2003 $10
Edited by Bertha Rogers
With commentary by Rory Golden & Keith Smith

Bright Hill Book Arts 2002 $10
Edited by Bertha Rogers
With commentary by Richard Minsky & Peter Verheyen

Ordering Bright Hill Press Books

BOOKSTORES & INDIVIDUALS: Bright Hill Press books are distributed to the trade and to the public by Small Press Distribution (spdbooks.com), 1341 Seventh Street Berkeley, CA 94710-1409; Baker & Taylor, 44 Kirby Ave., POB 734, Somerville, NJ 08876-0734; and North Country Books (regional titles), 311 Turner St., POB 217, Utica, NY 13501-1727. Our books may also be found at BN.com, Amazon.com, at your local bookstores, and at Bright Hill Press's website, brighthillpress.org (payment may be made by credit card and/or through PayPal). If your local bookstores do not stock Bright Hill Press books, please ask them to special order, or write to us at Bright Hill Press, 94 Church Street, Treadwell, NY 13846-4607 or to our e-mail address: wordthur@stny.rr.com, or call at 607-829-5055. Further information may be found on our website: brighthillpress.org; or by calling 607-829-5055.